The views expressed in this book are entirely those of the author.
All disputes are subject to arbitration, and legal actions, if any, are subject to the jurisdiction of courts at New Delhi, India.

A Special Message

Dear Reader,
I am blessed to have you reading
this.
Of what use is the shade of a tree,
If no traveler rests beneath it?
Of what use is the flower's
fragrance,
If no one ever delights in it?
For whatever exists here and now,
Is enriched by benefitting another.
Such are these lines of mine,
Kindles love and faith,
As in reading, as in writing.

Gift Of Gratitude

Please click on the link below to claim your gift.

https://www-sapnadeb-com-2.ck.page/03c82df262

A Silent Prayer

I offer my trouble, pain, and
misery,
 At your lotus feet, My God.
For the burden is heavy,
And my heart is breaking.

Your love for me is deep,
And your power infinite,
Heal my heart as I sleep,
With your magic wand.

You make mist of thorns,
You heal with your love,
May each day of mine,
Be an offering at your feet.

TABLE OF CONTENTS

Introduction

This is the sequel to my earlier book named **How to Create Positive Emotions.**

I am sure those of you who have read this and practiced along in the **Workbook on How to Create Positive Emotions** have already embarked on the journey to perennial happiness.

Life is a medley of circumstances which are not always in our favour. That is natural and right, for the benevolent Creator must take every child of his into consideration and that includes all living beings. Have we already not tilted the balance heavily towards human kind already? Are we not only concerned with ourselves, our welfare, and our interests to the exclusion of the rest of the creation? Isn't it ironic that it is this Rest of The CREATION that sustains us lovingly?

Our muscles become strong when we use them and so do our teeth when we use them to grind our food. Our mental muscles grow when we use them under trying circumstances, with awareness and courage. It takes fortitude and faith to stand tall under adverse circumstances. Every experience, circumstance and emotion are teachers who come to impart lessons. Welcome them and see what best you can do with them. As the mystic and my Guru, Sadhguru says, **"You can either become wise or wounded. You Can Choose What You Want to be."**

Is that not a blessing? This book will try to shine light on the ways to nurse our wounds and become wise as we go along our ways.

It is only this wisdom that we can carry to our afterlife. Not the mansion, not the swanky car, not the friends....

To the Mansion of God, our original, ancestral home, we return the way we had come, alone and with empty hands.

CHAPTER 1: The Cookery Show

That show was popular, and I tried not to miss it. Each contestant was given ingredients to mix and match and cook up a delicacy. It was sheer delight to watch them come up with innovative recipes that looked appetizing. The most delicious ones chosen by the three judges won the prize.

The mind is biased. It likes and dislikes. A tilted head, an endearing smile, a touch of humor, innocent eyes, a handsome face, and a soft corner develops swiftly in the heart. Albert was from Goa, and he was the most popular contestant on the show. He carried the salty sea air, the sunshine, and the music around him. His recipes were strange and exhilarating but that day was simply not his.
He stared at the cucumber and the lettuce and the scant spices that was handed over to him. What novel recipe could he possibly churn out of such uninteresting sparse ingredients? The clock does not stop ticking.

He lost that day. The dumpling of lettuce leaves he had made with cucumber and cheese filling did not go well with the taste buds of the judges. Then came the time of prize distribution and he was given a dressing down of wheat flour. So much of it was poured on him, that only his eyes remained twinkling. Since it was all done in good humor with a lot of laughter and mirth, he joined in the merriment too.
What have you got on your plate of life? Is it sparse as compared to others around you? Are you getting

'floured' by others for not being good enough? Is that eroding your self-esteem? Are you enjoying the experience?

Be calm if you are not.
It is just one scene of your life, a flash in time. Many other scenes will follow, and they will be better.

CHAPTER 2: The Play of The Senses

The headline in the newspaper left me sad and disgusted. A four-year-old girl had been gangraped and left to die in a ditch. The scene came painfully alive in front of my eyes and as I went about the morning chores hurriedly, the scene kept on replaying in my mind's eye. How could demons walk this earth in the garb of humans? Were humans demons beneath their harmless exterior?

Have you noticed what we see, listen, or hear especially in the morning be it on the television, radio, face book or Instagram affects the nature of our thoughts throughout the day. The mind cannot grow happy and peaceful thoughts when it feeds on negative thoughts throughout the day, especially in the morning. After many such instances, I keep away from the news. My work does not demand a good knowledge of that, and I consider myself fortunate.

I find peace and joy every morning by listening to calm, peaceful, spiritual talks or listening to soothing music as I go about my mornings every day. It keeps me charged with positive energy and rearing to go back to my patients. How can I heal if my own mind is at dis-ease? How can I charge another's energy if my own needs some recharging? *Every interaction with another human being is basically a transfer of energy.*

The entrance to the school was crowded with people. Mothers, fathers, grandfathers, grandmothers, and maids waited to take back their children home. I waited a little away from everyone. I am claustrophobic. There was a middle- aged man in the crowd. I do not know why I kept looking at him. He did not seem human though he was one in every way. My mind was inundated with pigs when I looked at him…

My mind sometimes acted so strangely that I felt that I should have nothing to do with it. But then mind is our constant companion and try as you may, you can never run away from it. So, keep it in a way that it makes a fulfilling companion to you, not an energy depleting one. Never make a PARASITE out of it, for it will suck out all the juices out of your life, leaving you high and dry.

Have you heard about the three monkeys of Mahatma Gandhi? They were his favourite toys. These monkeys embody a proverbial Japanese maxim.

Mizaru, the first one, covers his eyes to indicate that you should SEE NO EVIL.

Kikazaru, the second one, covers his ears to indicate that you should HEAR NO EVIL.

Iwazaru, the third monkey, covers his mouth to indicate that you should SPEAK NO EVIL.

We can add two others to it. Be careful of *what you EAT and DRINK*

At times, my colleagues go out for attending conferences or meetings to distant places. After they return, for a few days, they look distinctly different. After that, they are back to their original selves. One can recognize a tourist just by looking at him, even if he is dressed in a similar fashion. I had always wondered at it. It of course, had to do with their energy but what exactly made them so?

One day, I was listening to a talk by Sister Shivani, the famed spiritual teacher of the Brahma Kumaris. She said that in the earlier days, people used to ask a visitor, "You drink the water of which place?"
This was in lieu of the question, "Which place do you belong to?"
Water has memories and it is a quick absorber of vibrational energies. Once pervaded by the predominant energy of a place, it flows into the system of everyone, infusing them with it. Is it strange then, that people of a particular place resemble each other in some way or the other?

I am reminded of my school days. St. Joseph convent was my alma mater and we students could recognize one another on a faraway street even when not in uniform. We carry the energies of the place we stay in for long hours. Water is one of the major contributing factors to it.

The energy it carries may not always be beneficial. In ancient Indian homes, water was stored in a big earthen container overnight and prayers were offered to it in the morning before partaking of it. Research has proved that out thoughts can affect the water we hold in our glasses. Drink it with gratitude after seeking the blessings of God. It will then act in a different manner in the body. Water is the harbinger of life.

The water was boiling. Steam rose vigorously out of it, touching the ceiling and cascading down in a mist. The chef cut ginger, tomato, and capsicum into juliennes as he spoke enthusiastically about the tasty dish he was preparing. There is nothing as tasty as this when you put them straight into hot boiling water. Then the camera focused on what waited there for cooking. Five set of fearful eyes looked straight at it, and then the next moment they were shoved into the boiling water...

"Pluck and throw out the shells and enjoy."

Fear and anger tastes delicious. But what happens when the chemical markers of these emotions, present in the food, courses through the veins?

It turned out later, that my mind was not strange. I realized that I should continue my deep camaraderie with it.

"My father loves pork. None of his meals are complete without five to ten pieces of it. I must leave early, you know. I need to buy some of it," My friend said, pointing to the middle-aged man, her father.

My jaw fell open.

What building blocks do you use for making your body? Whatever they might be, always remember that you will radiate that energy.

CHAPTER 3: Deep Sleep

The road was steep. I was panting as I carried my unwilling legs and a revolting heart throbbing restlessly within me. I did not want to be a part of this village hospital. I had freshly passed out of medical school and was starry eyed. This joining order had come out of the blue. I was totally unprepared.

The house was big. A balcony in front and behind, the walls of which were crisscrossed wooden bars. The rooms were big and so was the kitchen. I felt lonely and lost. I was used to the protected hostel life with fun and frolic and friends snuggling together at night. There is something warm about the company of friends. One felt cozy in that cocoon.
There was a courtyard behind enclosed by a backwall.

"What is there behind it?" I asked pointing to the door made on the wall. It had become a part of the wall and did not seem to have an existence of its own. That was strange.
"Never open that door," the guard said.
There was a warning look in his eyes.
"Why cannot I open that door?" I asked defiantly.
"There is a thick jungle behind which extends for many acres and acres. The wild animals there are not good," he said with a shrug of his shoulders.
"That is why they made that wall so high, you know," he added.

The guard left soon after. Here was I, amid a jungle all alone in a house, which was so far away from that of the other staff, that my cry for help in my loudest voice would fall on deaf ears.

I went to the hospital after dropping my things and by the time I came back the sky had started to turn dark. The two attendants helped me in arranging the sparse things I had and then left hurriedly.

I retired for the night and then the performance began of the unseen. I heard growls and cries so near my window that I almost jumped out of my skin. I dare not go near the window to close it. I took my pillow and quilt to the other windowless large room and sat quietly. And then started the mad laughter and the crying and the howling...

I nearly howled myself. I dare not go to the door for who knew what waited outside for me?
It was about 3 a.m. when the orchestra stopped, and I thought I would just go to the nurse and request her to let me sleep in their house. I went to the front room when I stopped in my tracks. A huge man stood motionless, outlined against the window trying to peek in...

I endured this drama almost every day for two long years. I worked all day and dropped tired to the bed all night, wary and sleepless. My ears were always open trying to catch the unwelcome sound of someone entering the house. No one did but a frightened mind makes its own ghosts. In my case, they added to it.

I had transformed by then. My anxious mind could not sit still. Tired and listless, I became suspicious and nervous. Such was the state of my mind that I could not understand what to do next. I could not concentrate and cried over little things uncontrollably. I wished to run away every day but could not. Making a simple decision seemed a horrendous task. Of all that crippled me during that time, ambivalence was on the top of the list.

The foxes, the jackals and the hyenas had done the trick. It may be noted that I was neither having delusions not hallucinations as said in medical parlance. Fear and lack of sleep had caused my mental state. Recovery was immediate and complete, once I left that place for good.

Sleep plays a very important role in healing our body from the wear and tear during the day. Have you noticed how drained of all energy you feel if you have not slept well the night before?

Sleep allows various physiological and biochemical mechanisms to repair tissues, regenerate cells and strengthen the immune system. It is essential for overall health and well-being, impacting various cognitive functions, including emotional regulation. Among the different stages of sleep, deep sleep, also known as slow-wave sleep, plays a crucial role in emotional processing and regulation.

Emotional Processing During Deep Sleep
During deep sleep, the brain undergoes important processes that help in emotional regulation. Research

suggests that the brain consolidates memories and processes emotional information during this stage. This consolidation is vital for managing emotions effectively during waking hours.

Impact on Mood Regulation
Deep sleep is linked to mood regulation and emotional stability. Studies have shown that individuals who experience deep sleep disturbances are more likely to have mood disorders and difficulties in regulating emotions. This highlights the importance of deep sleep in maintaining emotional balance.

Stress Management and Emotional Resilience
Deep sleep is essential for stress management and building emotional resilience. Adequate deep sleep allows the brain to reset and recover, enabling individuals to cope better with stressors and emotional challenges. Lack of deep sleep can lead to heightened emotional reactivity and difficulties in managing stress.

Neurobiological Mechanisms
Neurobiological mechanisms underlying the relationship between deep sleep and emotional regulation involve the processing of emotional memories, the regulation of stress hormones, and the maintenance of neurotransmitter balance. These mechanisms are crucial for maintaining emotional well-being.

Clinical Implications

Sleep disturbances, particularly disruptions in deep sleep, have been associated with various emotional disorders such as depression, anxiety, and mood disorders. Addressing sleep problems, including enhancing deep sleep quality, is essential in the treatment and management of emotional disturbances. I developed obesity and hypothyroidism during my time there. When you do not sleep enough, your body undergoes changes to prove it.

How can we ensure deep sleep?
My childhood days were filled with fun and frolic. It was also laced with discipline. At the stroke of 8.45 p.m., we children would set aside our books and run to the kitchen table, in preparation of dinner. One of us cut the salad, while another filled the jugs and glasses, and another got the plates ready. Dinner started at the stroke of 9 p.m. and after the chores, we all were on our beds by 10 p.m.

I could still hear the other children playing while their parents strolled about. I wished they would sleep too. We would have to be up by 4.45 a.m. and then go for a walk with my father. My youngest sibling was four years then.

We set out when the sky was still dark. The chilling cut in the air, the quiet and the darkness bored into our being. The silence and the peace seeped into our beings. We saw the stars fade away as the sky paled, the orange sky hugging the earth far away. My heart yearned to reach the spot where the earth enveloped the sky in its bosom. Then little birds chirped, the trees swayed while the dew drops sparkled. It was time to retrace my steps back home. But this was home; this wilderness and beauty was my home. It still is...

This consistency of sleep timing is pertinent to enhance deep sleep and promote emotional regulation. One can adopt healthy sleep habits such as creating a relaxing bedtime routine, ensuring a comfortable sleep environment, and avoiding stimulants before bedtime.

Deep sleep plays a vital role in emotional regulation by facilitating emotional processing, mood regulation, stress management, and emotional resilience. Physical well- being can be ensured only if emotional well- being is present. Prioritizing deep sleep is essential for **transforming negative emotions** resulting in overall wellness.

CHAPTER 4: Let Go

If you love somebody, let them go,
For if they return, they were always yours.
And if they don't, they never were.
Kahlil Gibran.

 Elizabeth Gilbert is best known for her memoir, **"Eat, Pray, Love."** After facing a devastating divorce and a subsequent relationship breakdown, Gilbert found herself entangled in depression and confusion about her life and future. Her journey of letting go and healing is a living proof of the transformative power of releasing sad memories and the associated pain.

The Process of Letting Go:
Gilbert's process of letting go began with the acknowledgment of her unhappiness and the acceptance that she could not continue living her life as it was. *Have we not ourselves felt so many a time? The invisible burden of sad memories eats into our being, dissipating all joy and peace.* This realization led her to make a radical decision to leave behind her existing life in search of self-discovery and healing. She embarked on a year-long journey around the world, which became the foundation of her memoir.

Finding Healing:
    Eat (Italy) –
 Gilbert's journey started in Italy, where she embraced the pleasure of nourishment, allowing herself to enjoy

food and learn Italian, focusing on the joy of living in the moment. This step was crucial in her process of letting go of her past self-criticism and embracing self-care and pleasure.

How often we are lost in another world as food goes down our throats! Living in the moment helps us savour the food and feel gratitude for the lives that are being sacrificed to sustain us.

2. **Pray (India)** - The next phase of her journey took her to an ashram in India, where she explored the depths of spirituality and meditation. Here, Gilbert engaged in the painstaking work of facing her inner demons, forgiving herself and those around her, and letting go of the heavy burdens she had been carrying. This period was marked by significant introspection and spiritual growth. *How redeeming it is to drop a heavy bundle which pricks, leaving us bent and bleeding. Drop it and run as fast as you can. It might have fallen in love with you in all these years and might try to perch on your back again.*

3. **Love (Bali, Indonesia)** - Finally, in Bali, Gilbert sought to balance the pleasures of the world with spiritual enlightenment. It was here that she unexpectedly found love again, not by searching for it, but by allowing herself to be open and vulnerable. This love came only after she had released her previous conceptions of love and relationships, demonstrating the beauty that can follow when one truly lets it go.

Have you seen how fast sand disappears from clenched hands? When our hands are open and steady, a butterfly can alight on it and spread her beautiful wings.

Letting go of past identities, pain, and grief can lead to profound healing and unexpected new beginnings. Forgiving does not mean what the other person had done to harm, was right. It means that you no longer allow the memories of that event to cause you pain. You set yourself free.

Elizabeth's journey teaches us that sometimes, to find peace and happiness, we must be willing to release what we hold onto so tightly, be it a relationship, a job, or even a place. She was able to heal and transform her life in ways she never imagined by forgiving and releasing the past and painful memories associated with it, embracing change, and surrendering to a higher power.

Her experience depicts the importance of self-love, the pursuit of inner peace, and the courage to embark on new paths. Her best -selling book continues to inspire many who find themselves at crossroads, reminding them of the *resilience* of the human spirit and that *negative emotions can be transformed* by releasing them.

CHAPTER 5: Have no Expectations

To be human means to be capable of being conscious about everything that you do.
Sadhguru

Letting go of expectations brings immense freedom, peace, and fulfillment in our lives. Expectations, often rooted in our desires, assumptions, and societal norms, can become heavy burdens that limit our happiness and peace of mind.

The Weight of Expectations

Expectations are like invisible chains that bind us to specific outcomes, behaviors, or conditions we believe we or others should meet. Whether it's the pressure to excel in our careers, maintain perfect relationships, or adhere to societal standards of success, expectations can create stress, anxiety, and disappointment when reality doesn't align with our imagined ideals.

The Art of Letting Go

Letting go of expectations is a conscious choice to release our attachment to specific outcomes and embrace life as it unfolds. We need to surrender our need for control, accept uncertainty, and trust the natural flow of existence. Once we free ourselves from the shackles of expectations, endless possibilities and opportunities for growth and joy open.

Benefits of Having no Expectations

Freedom and Peace:
When we have no expectations, we liberate ourselves from the confines of should and musts. This allows us to experience a sense of freedom and peace. We can find serenity in the present moment by accepting things as they are.

Improved Relationships:
Most relationships develop chinks and fail because expectations of those involved in it were not met. Releasing expectations in relationships brings about deeper connections and authentic interactions. When we have no preconceived notions of how others should behave or how relationships should unfold, we create space for understanding, empathy, and acceptance, leading to more harmonious and fulfilling connections. Most of the times, the significant other has no idea about the expectations we have and hence does not act in accordance.

Enhanced Mental Wellbeing:
Having no expectations reduces stress, anxiety, and feelings of inadequacy. When we shift our focus from rigid outcomes to appreciating the journey and the process, we cultivate a sense of gratitude, resilience, and inner peace.

Personal Growth and Resilience:
Having no expectations can be a catalyst for personal growth and self -discovery. It challenges us to step outside our comfort zones, adapt to change, and welcome new experiences with courage and openness.

This in turn helps us in developing greater resilience and adaptability.

Increased Joy and Fulfillment:
By releasing expectations and living in the present moment, we can find joy and fulfillment in the simple pleasures of life. We can appreciate the beauty and richness of each moment, finding contentment in the here and now.

Living in the Present Moment:
Releasing expectations is a continual practice that requires mindfulness, self-awareness, and compassion. It's about being present, accepting what is, and letting go of the need for things to be a certain way. We then cultivate a deep sense of gratitude, acceptance, and inner peace that transcends the limitations of our own expectations. Is that not wonderful?

CHAPTER 6: Negative emotions

Life is a set of experiences, and they give rise to emotions. Some of them are seen as beneficial while there are others which are not so, especially if indulged in for longer periods. ***The latter come to signal and motivate, to teach and to communicate, to save and protect.*** It is the yearning for survival, this fight, flight and freeze response. It is this which has maintained the species of humankind from time immemorial. We are not adorning the annals of history along with the dinosaurs because of this primal, basic instinct.

But this basic survival instinct response is to propel us into action. What if action at that optimum level is not required? What if there is no reason to fight, flight or freeze? The mind creates the thought and in response the body creates chemical messengers to bring about the appropriate response. If there is no action taken, what do you think happens to the plethora of the chemical messengers let loose in the system? What if this is done again and again? What if this becomes a habit?

Stress and Anxiety:
Chronic stress and anxiety can lead to a range of health problems, including cardiovascular issues, weakened immune system, and digestive disorders. A study published in the Journal of Health Psychology found that people with higher levels of anxiety experienced

more physical symptoms and reported lower overall well-being.

Anger and Hostility:

Frequent outbursts of anger and hostility have been linked to increased risks of heart disease, high blood pressure, and weakened immune system. Research conducted at the University of Massachusetts Medical School suggests that anger and hostility can contribute to the development of chronic diseases and have negative effects on overall health.

Sadness and Depression:

Prolonged sadness and depression can impact both physical and mental health, leading to fatigue, disrupted sleep patterns, changes in appetite, and reduced immune function. A study published in the Journal of Clinical Psychology found that individuals with depressive symptoms had higher rates of chronic health conditions and reported lower quality of life.

Fear and Phobias:

Fear and phobias trigger the body's stress response, leading to increased heart rate, rapid breathing, and elevated blood pressure. Research at the University of Texas at Austin suggests that chronic fear and phobias can contribute to the development of anxiety disorders and have long-lasting effects on mental health.

Guilt and Shame:

Experiencing frequent guilt and shame can have detrimental effects on mental health, leading to increased levels of stress, anxiety, and decreased self-esteem. Studies have shown that experiencing chronic guilt was associated with higher levels of depressive symptoms and lower overall well-being.

Jealousy and Envy:
Jealousy and envy can cause significant emotional distress and impact relationships. Individuals who frequently experienced jealousy reported higher levels of depression and anxiety.

All the above prove that negative emotions, invariably bring about great harm if indulged in repeatedly and for a long time. It becomes a habit which erodes physical as well as mental well-being and invites a horde of diseases.

Why is it that the same situation evokes different emotions in different individuals? Why is it that the same situation evokes different emotions in the same individual at different times?
We might get angry on our children if they are rude. But will we be angry if the Boss is rude? We will still be at our best behavior despite it, for the fear of being fired.
That indicates that we decide when to respond with anger.

Why not train our minds to respond after some deliberation than to react immediately?

CHAPTER 7: Stress and Anxiety

Stress and anxiety have become increasingly prevalent in today's fast-paced world. In this chapter, we will discuss the causes of stress and anxiety, explore their symptoms, and impact on our lives as well as discuss coping mechanisms.

Work and Academic Pressure:
It is a fast-paced world, and high workloads, tight deadlines, and academic demands can contribute to stress and anxiety. Feeling overwhelmed or lacking control over tasks can intensify these emotions. One inadvertently becomes a part of this mad rat race.

Life Transitions and Uncertainty:
It is said that Change is the only constant in life, but it never fails to catch one unawares. Major life changes, such as moving, changing jobs, or ending relationships, can trigger stress and anxiety. Uncertainty about the future or fear of the unknown can exacerbate these feelings.

Financial Challenges:
Financial difficulties, debt, or job insecurity can create significant stress and anxiety. Worrying about meeting basic needs or maintaining a certain lifestyle can take a toll on both, physical as well as mental well-being.

Health Concerns:
Chronic illnesses, physical pain, or concerns about one's health can lead to stress and anxiety. Coping with medical treatments, managing symptoms, and

uncertainty about the future can contribute to these emotions.

Unrealistic Expectations:
Everyone seems to be striving for excellence and financial stardom. That big house, that car, that exotic vacation … the list is endless. More achievements lead to more money and more hunger for the same. It is a vicious cycle. Where does this end?

Stress and Anxiety can impact in various ways.

Emotional Symptoms:
The next time you walk, observe the people around you. **You will notice that most people are lost in their own sad world**. Some look overwhelmed, some angry or worried. Feeling irritable, easily agitated, experiencing persistent worry, fear, or difficulty concentrating are symptoms of stress. Frequent mood swings, restlessness, or a sense of impending doom point towards the same.

Physical Symptoms:
Headaches, muscle tension, and aches, fatigue, insomnia, changes in appetite, digestive problems, including stomachaches or nausea are physical symptoms.

Impact on Daily Life:
Chronic stress and anxiety can affect various areas of life, including work performance, relationships, and physical health. They can lead to social withdrawal, decreased productivity, a reduced quality of life, depression, and suicidal tendencies.

Almost one in fourteen people suffer from this and it is one of the major mental health problems in the world. So, you are not alone if you feel you are anxious all the time.

Anxiety helps in dealing with life situations. It has been found that those who have coping skills and better control over their lives, do not suffer the teachings of this teacher. Those who are not equipped with them and have lesser control over their lives, worry about everything and go down the spiral of anxiety.

What are the coping mechanisms which one can equip oneself with? There are various strategies to cope with stress and anxiety.

Anything worth doing is worth doing well is an oft repeated adage but this is exactly what leads to anxiety.

Will I be able to do this well? Will people judge me if I fail to do this well? Will I fall in my own eyes if I do not live up to my expectations? My expectations are usually lofty, and I wish to shine for all to see. I am a perfectionist but of course, I do not know or if I know, I do not like to accept that.

I had always wanted to be a writer, but I kept on postponing it. I had trained to be a surgeon, not a writer. My language skills were that of a sixth- grade student. I did not have a vivid imagination so I could write only about the mere happenings in my life. Who would be interested in that?

That all changed when I started writing and realized that it is the ordinary that is interesting. My articles had scope of improvement and the more I wrote, the better I became. It was then that I understood what G. K. Chesterton meant when he said the following line.

1. **"Anything worth doing is worth doing badly."**

This is the first coping strategy. It takes the fear of failing away and prods you to take that one shaky step. It fills you with anticipation and excitement. You now have your sight set on doing whatever is needed than on the result of your action.

You have the right to work,
But never to the fruit thereof,
You should neither engage in action,
For the sake of a reward,
Nor should you long for inaction.

Bhagavad Gita

2. *Become an observer:*

Our brains are wired for survival. One cannot run away from anxiety. Who can run away from his own mind? So, play some mind games.

Imagine yourself as bird flying out of your body and perching on the ceiling. Watch yourself. You have now created a distance from your body and have become an observer. The view from above is clearer and can be seen in its entirety.

What is the cause? What are the factors causing it? Is it so much to worry about? Am I overestimating the problem? Am I expecting a catastrophic result which has little chance of occurring? What can be done about it?

When you look at it like a detached observer, the giant becomes a cat.

3. Practice Self-love:

We tend to be kind and loving to all around but strangely forget to do the same for ourselves. Serving others before self, places us at a self-anointed pedestal which polishes our ego. Gratitude of others makes us feel good about ourselves and reinforces our own positive image in our own eyes.

Make yourself the fulcrum of your own life. Be your own sun. Take care of yourself, attend to your needs, and do what you feel good doing.

Make a list of all things you did today which made you feel happy and which you could do on your own without outside help. Seek your own approval and not that of others. Slowly you will realize that you are getting better at doing your own things and your life is under your control. Then your emotions and feelings will be under your control too. Research has shown that new neural pathways develop once you walk this path of self-love and appreciation, long enough. Your overtly anxious self will be left far behind.

4. Practice Yoga asanas:

Yoga asanas affects the mind in such a manner that negative and anxious thoughts are kept at bay. Regular practice heals the body and mind and connects one with the universal consciousness. When your discharged batteries are connected to the super charger of the creator, you always remain charged to the optimum.

5. Read a motivational/ Spiritual book every day before sleeping:

What is your favourite book?

The books of Swami Yogananda are my favourite. Do read the Autobiography of The Yogi and Man's Eternal Quest by him. The chapters have a strange way of bringing God near you. It is as if one can extend his arm and touch him. I feel safe in his presence every night. With him near me, I have no cause to worry.

Besides the above, the following can be done.
- Engage in regular exercise, eat a balanced diet, and prioritize sufficient sleep.
- Break tasks into manageable steps and set realistic goals.
- Prioritize tasks based on importance and urgency to reduce overwhelm.
- Seek support from friends, family, or support groups.
-Share your feelings and concerns with trusted individuals who can provide a listening ear and perspective.

Stress and anxiety are common experiences that significantly impact our well-being and daily lives. Dwell upon the causes and recognize the symptoms of stress and anxiety to manage it effectively. By implementing **coping strategies,** we can tide over these mental states and cultivate **resilience.** Everyone's journey is unique, and finding what works best for us is the key.

CHAPTER 8: Anger and Hostility

"Holding on to anger is like drinking poison and expecting the other person to die."
- ***Gautama Buddha***

Anger and hostility are intense emotions that can have profound effects on our mental and physical well-being. We will learn about the symptoms of anger and hostility, their potential impact on our health, and effective strategies to manage and cope with these emotions.

Symptoms of Anger and Hostility

Emotional Symptoms:
One feels intense anger, irritability, or frustration, a sense of injustice, resentment, or bitterness or has difficulty in controlling anger outbursts or impulsivity.

Physical Symptoms:
An individual's heart rate and blood pressure increases, muscle tension, headaches, clenched jaws, sweating, and trembling occurs. Unless the anger is directed towards you, a dancing angry man looks funny, isn't it?

Behavioral Symptoms:
An angry man displays aggressive behavior, such as yelling, shouting, or physical aggression.

Health Impacts of Anger and Hostility

Cardiovascular Issues:

Chronic anger and hostility have been linked to an increased risk of heart disease, high blood pressure, and stroke. Prolonged exposure to these emotions can lead to the development of atherosclerosis and contribute to cardiovascular problems.

Weakened Immune System:
Persistent anger and hostility can weaken the immune system, making individuals more susceptible to infections and illnesses. Research suggests that individuals with high levels of anger experience slower wound healing and have compromised immune responses.

Mental Health Challenges:
Uncontrolled anger and hostility can contribute to the development of mental health disorders, such as depression and anxiety. These emotions can also strain relationships, exacerbating feelings of loneliness.

Coping Strategies for Anger and Hostility

Recognize and Acknowledge Anger:
One needs to study oneself and understand the triggers and clues that lead to anger and hostility. Then practice self-awareness and recognize the early signs of escalating anger to nip it in the bud.

Relaxation Techniques:
One can engage in deep breathing exercises, progressive muscle relaxation, or meditation to calm the mind and body. Yoga and mindfulness practices can also help to manage anger and promote emotional well-being.

Cognitive Restructuring:

Try to challenge negative thought patterns and replace them with more rational and positive thoughts. Reframe situations to gain a different perspective and reduce anger-provoking interpretations. Write down your thoughts during such times. It helps to gain a better perspective of the functioning of your own mind.

Communication and Conflict Resolution:

Effective communication skills can help to remove the bite of anger. A calm tone and respectful mannerisms do not hurt anyone. Seek healthy outlets to express emotions, such as journaling or talking to a trusted friend or therapist.

Seek Professional Help:

If anger and hostility are significantly impacting your life and relationships, consider seeking therapy or counseling. Cognitive-behavioral therapy (CBT) and anger management programs can provide valuable tools for managing and coping with anger.

Heal the energy body:

One of the best ways to transform negative emotions is to heal the energy body and thereby the physical body. When the energy body is well and glowing, the mind is in an equanimous state.

CHAPTER 9: Sadness and Depression

Watch your thoughts, they become your words.
Watch your words, they become your actions.
Watch your actions, they become your habits.
Watch your habits, they become your character.
Watch your character, it becomes your destiny.
-Lao Tzu

The importance of having right thoughts cannot be over emphasized. How often do we blame our destiny for the situations in our life. Destiny has not been imposed on us. We have created it each day, little by little. Sadness and depression are also caused by this downward spiral of thoughts, and it can significantly impact our mental and physical well-being.

Causes of Sadness and Depression

Biological Factors:
Imbalances in brain chemistry, genetics, or hormonal changes can contribute to the development of depression. Research suggests that certain individuals may have a genetic predisposition to depression.

Environmental Factors:
Traumatic life events, such as loss, abuse, or chronic stress, can trigger feelings of sadness and lead to depression. Lack of social support, financial difficulties, and relationship problems can also contribute to these emotions.

Cognitive Factors:

Negative thinking patterns, low self-esteem, and distorted perceptions of oneself and the world can contribute to the development of depression. Ruminating on negative experiences and having a pessimistic outlook can further intensify feelings of sadness.

Symptoms and Impact of Sadness and Depression

Emotional Symptoms:
There can be persistent feelings of sadness, emptiness, or hopelessness. This is coupled with loss of interest or pleasure in activities once enjoyed. There is an increase in irritability, restlessness and crying spells.

Cognitive Symptoms:
Concentrating, making decisions, or remembering details become difficult. The mind is inundated with negative thoughts, self-criticism, or feelings of worthlessness. There is an increase in suicidal thoughts or preoccupation with death.

Physical Symptoms:
The body feels fatigued, energy and motivation are low. Changes in appetite, weight loss, or weight gain can be seen. This is accompanied by sleep disturbances like insomnia or excessive sleepiness.

Impact on the Body:
Depression has been associated with various physical health issues, including cardiovascular disease, diabetes, and weakened immune system. Studies have shown that individuals with depression may have

higher levels of inflammation and altered immune functioning.

Coping Strategies for Sadness and Depression

Practice Yoga Asanas:
There is nothing as effective as doing ancient and time-tested yoga asanas every day. Set out at least an hour every day in the morning and be at peace every day, despite the trial and the tribulations you encounter.

Seek Professional Help:
Reach out to a mental health professional who can provide guidance, support, and evidence-based treatments for depression. Psychotherapy, such as cognitive-behavioral therapy (CBT), can help identify and challenge negative thoughts and develop coping strategies.

Build a Support System:
Friends are our umbrellas during rainy days. Surround yourself with supportive friends, family, or support groups who can provide understanding and encouragement. Sharing your feelings and experiences with others can help alleviate feelings of loneliness and isolation. Have you experienced how light you feel when you get it out of your chest? How can the lungs inflate with a deflating load on it?

Self- Care:
Engage in activities that bring you joy and provide a sense of fulfillment. Prioritize self-care by getting regular exercise, eating a balanced diet, sleeping well, and practicing relaxation techniques.

Mindfulness and Meditation:
Practice mindfulness-based techniques, such as meditation or deep breathing exercises, to cultivate self-awareness and reduce negative thoughts and emotions. Research has shown that there is a direct link between the way we breathe, and our emotional status.

Yogic philosophy mentions that we are given a *particular number of breaths when we dawn on this earth. The counting starts from the time you first cried at birth.* Breathe slow, my friend, and long. Why do you want to hasten your exit from this world? This world is beautiful...

CHAPTER 10: Fear and Phobias

Fear and phobias are common emotions that can impact our daily lives and well-being.

Causes of Fear and Phobias

Learned Responses:
Fear can be a learned response through traumatic experiences or witnessing others' fearful reactions. Phobias often develop from a specific triggering event or experience, leading to an exaggerated fear response. A child who has hurt himself by fire learns to fear it as an adult as well.

Biological Factors:
Some individuals may have a genetic predisposition to developing phobias. Brain chemistry and specific brain regions involved in fear and anxiety responses may contribute to the development of phobias.

Environmental Factors:
Growing up in an environment where fear is reinforced or where safety and security are compromised can increase the likelihood of developing phobias. Cultural and societal influences can also play a role in the development of specific phobias.

Symptoms and Impact of Fear and Phobias

Emotional Symptoms:
There is intense fear, panic, or anxiety when encountering the feared object or situation. It can also present as persistent and irrational worry or

anticipation of encountering the feared object or situation. Avoidance behaviors to prevent exposure to the feared object or situation can be seen too.

Physical Symptoms:
There can be rapid heartbeat, shortness of breath, chest tightness, sweating, trembling, feeling lightheaded, nausea, stomach discomfort, or dizziness.

Impact on Daily Life:
Fear and phobias can significantly limit one's activities and experiences. They can lead to social isolation, difficulty maintaining relationships, and hinder personal and professional growth.

Coping Strategies for Fear and Phobias

Gradual Exposure:
Gradually expose yourself to the feared object or situation in a controlled and safe manner. Start with less anxiety-provoking situations and gradually work your way up to more challenging ones.

Cognitive-Behavioral Therapy (CBT):
Seek professional help from a therapist trained in CBT to identify and challenge irrational thoughts and beliefs associated with fear and phobias. This can help develop effective coping strategies and change behavioral patterns.

Relaxation Techniques:
Practice relaxation techniques such as deep breathing, progressive muscle relaxation, or meditation to manage anxiety and promote a sense of well-being.

Professional Intervention:

In severe cases, medication prescribed by a healthcare professional may be beneficial to alleviate symptoms and manage anxiety related to fear and phobias. It is important to work closely with a healthcare provider to determine the most appropriate course of action.

CHAPTER 11: Guilt and Shame

Tonight, I see the realm of joy and pleasure,
I have lost myself in it.
And it has lost itself in me:
No religion,
No dogma,
No conformity,
No guilt,
No shame,
No fear,
No conviction,
No uncertainty remains.
In the middle of my heart,
A star appears,
And the seven heavens,
Are lost in its brilliance.
-Rumi

Guilt and shame are complex emotions that can have a profound impact on our mental and emotional well-being.

Causes of Guilt and Shame

Moral and Cultural Influences:
Guilt and shame can stem from internalizing societal or cultural norms and values. Moral conflicts or violations of personal or societal standards can trigger feelings of guilt and shame.

Personal Beliefs and Expectations:
Unrealistic or overly rigid personal beliefs and expectations can contribute to the experience of guilt

and shame. Holding oneself to impossible standards or feeling responsible for the actions or well-being of others can intensify these emotions.

Traumatic Experiences:
Experiencing or witnessing traumatic events, abuse, or violations can lead to deep-rooted feelings of guilt and shame. Survivors of trauma may internalize blame or responsibility for the event, resulting in overwhelming guilt and shame.

Symptoms and Impact of Guilt and Shame
Emotional Symptoms:
Overwhelming feelings of remorse, self-blame, or self-disgust may result in persistent feelings of worthlessness, unworthiness, or inadequacy. This in turn leads to anxiety, depression, or a sense of hopelessness.

Behavioral Symptoms:
They avoid situations, people, or activities that trigger feelings of guilt or shame. They engage in self-destructive behavior to cope with or punish themselves.

Impact on Self-Image and Relationships:
Guilt and shame can erode self-esteem and lead to a negative self-image. These emotions can strain relationships, as individuals may struggle with trust and genuine connection.

Coping Strategies for Guilt and Shame

Self-Compassion and Acceptance:

Be kind to yourself as you are to others. You surely deserve what you give off so freely. Practice self-compassion by acknowledging that everyone makes mistakes and that it is a part of being human. Do not judge yourself. Forgive the past and move ahead.

Cognitive Restructuring:
Always challenge negative and self-critical thoughts by examining evidence and considering alternative perspectives. Joseph Nguyen, best-selling author advises this in his book named **Don't believe everything you think**. Replace self-blame with self-compassionate and realistic thoughts.

Forgiveness:
Practice forgiveness towards oneself and others involved in the situation. Understand that forgiveness does not condone the actions, but it allows for healing and moving forward. When you forgive, you set yourself free.

Therapeutic Interventions:
Consider seeking therapy or counseling to work through deep-rooted guilt and shame. Therapeutic approaches such as cognitive-behavioral therapy (CBT), dialectical behavior therapy (DBT), or acceptance and commitment therapy (ACT) can be effective in addressing and resolving these emotions.

Hold your head high as a special child of the Creator. Why should guilt or shame torment your soul when you are in his care?

CHAPTER 12: Envy and Jealousy

If you love somebody, let them go,
for if they return, they were always yours.
If they don't, they never were.
-Kahlil Gibran

Envy is as old as mankind and almost every language in the world has a name for it. Envy and jealousy have been used interchangeably in common parlance, but they are not essentially the same. Jealousy is wanting to protect what you think is essentially yours like the love of your romantic partner. There is no shame involved in admitting it for there is social recognition that you are protecting that what is rightfully yours. Envy is complex and intricate for you crave for something that belongs to another, whether material or intangible. These emotions can cast dark shadows, causing turmoil within us and strain loving relationships.

The Roots of Envy and Jealousy

Envy and jealousy often stem from feelings of inadequacy, comparison, and fear. One may be envious of one's sibling, friend, or spouse.

In a world where achievements and possessions are celebrated, it is natural to fall into the trap of measuring our worth against others. Social media platforms, often portraying curated versions of people's lives, can exacerbate these feelings. They can arise from unmet desires or aspirations, leading us to resent those who seemingly have what we lack.

The Effects on the Body and Mind

They can have profound impacts on our well-being. Research shows that these negative emotions can trigger stress responses in the body, leading to increased heart rate, elevated blood pressure, and even compromised immune function. Mentally, envy and jealousy can consume our thoughts, breeding negativity, and eroding self-esteem. They can also strain relationships, fostering a toxic atmosphere of resentment and competition.

Achieving Emotional Freedom

Fortunately, there are ways to free ourselves from envy and jealousy. At the onset one needs to recognize it.

1. You have negative feelings for a person who has neither harmed nor hurt you in any way. In fact, that person might be understanding and loving towards you. (She looks so beautiful.)
2. You are mentally indulging in a competition with another person though the latter is unaware of it.
3. You love to hear others talk negatively about that person and add your own titbits to the gossip though they are untrue.

If the above are true, acknowledge to yourself that you are envious of that person. Acceptance is the first step towards healing.

Self-Reflection:

Engaging in honest self-reflection allows us to identify our insecurities and areas for personal growth. Embracing self-acceptance and understanding that everyone has their unique journey and destiny helps alleviate comparison-induced envy.

Cultivate Gratitude:
Practicing gratitude shifts our focus from what we lack to what we have. Regularly acknowledging and appreciating the blessings in our lives can help counteract envy.

Practice Empathy:
Developing empathy towards others allows us to celebrate their successes genuinely. Recognizing that someone else's achievements do not diminish our own can help dissolve feelings of envy.

Limit Social Media Engagement:
While social media can be a valuable tool for connection, excessive exposure can fuel envy and jealousy. Setting boundaries and being mindful of our online interactions can protect our mental well-being.

Focus on Personal Growth:
What you are envious of in another person, is what your innermost self is craving for you to do. Is this not a guiding light?

Envy calls upon you to understand that you are a unique creation of God and his treasure despite the inadequacies you imagine you have. He created you perfect and different from all others. Each of his creations are unique and serve their purpose best when they remain so and not try to imitate and emulate others. Imagine if a banana plant wished to become a mango tree and all the others also wanted to become so? Won't we all get tired of the mango then? We want the plants to be the way they were originally made. That is also the way they can serve their unique purpose.

You can serve your own unique purpose by being and remaining you. No one else can take your place. ***ONLY YOU HAVE THE POWER TO SHINE YOUR LIGHT THE BRIGHTEST.***

Reference: PSYCHE How to put envy to good use.

CHAPTER 13: The Trap of Hatred

When someone criticizes or disagrees with you,
A small ant of hatred and antagonism is born in your
heart.
If you do not squash the ant at once, it might grow
into a snake or even a dragon.
-Rumi

Hatred is a dragon, a powerful and destructive emotion, that has plagued humanity throughout history. It manifests in various forms, from personal animosity to deep-rooted prejudice and even societal conflicts. We will explore the complexities of hatred, its origins, psychological and societal impacts, and read about ways to foster understanding and compassion to counteract its effects in this chapter.,

The Nature of Hatred
Hatred is a multifaceted emotion that arises from a deep sense of anger, resentment, fear, or disgust towards individuals, groups, or even abstract concepts. It often stems from experiences of injustice, betrayal, or perceived threats to one's identity or values. Hatred can be fueled by ignorance, prejudice, or a desire for power, and it thrives in an environment that perpetuates division and dehumanization.

Psychological and Physiological Effects
Hatred has far-reaching effects on both individuals and societies. Psychologically, it consumes the mind, promoting negative thoughts and emotions, leading to increased stress, anxiety, and depression. It can distort one's perception, impair empathy, and hinder the

ability to form meaningful social connections. Chronic suppressed anger and hatred can contribute to elevated blood pressure, weakened immune function, and other adverse health outcomes. Some research papers have mentioned about it to be causing cancer.

Hatred's Impact on Society

Hatred's impact extends beyond the individual, permeating social structures and relationships. It fuels discrimination, prejudice, and violence, perpetuating cycles of harm and perpetuating deep-seated divisions. Hatred can lead to the marginalization and persecution of individuals or entire groups based on their race, religion, gender, or other characteristics. It undermines social cohesion, stifles progress, and poses a threat to peace and harmony within communities.

Countering Hatred with Compassion

While hatred may seem insurmountable, understanding, empathy, and compassion can act as potent antidotes. Here are some strategies to consider:

Education and Awareness:

Promoting education that fosters the knowledge that there is an underlying unity among all human beings is essential, right from an early age. The spirit in each, is the continuation of the universal spirit. Once each child knows this from an early age, he will know that there are no walls between the hearts of one another.

Waves of joy will then flow,
from one heart to another and so will tears.

Dialogue and Listening:

Engaging in open, respectful dialogue allows for the exchange of ideas and perspectives. Active listening enables the recognition of shared humanity, removing misunderstanding and facilitating compassion.

Cultivating Empathy:
Empathy involves acknowledging and sharing the feelings of others. By actively seeking to understand diverse experiences and perspectives, we can develop empathy and appreciate those we may have previously seen as enemies.

Promoting Social Justice:
Addressing systemic inequalities and advocating for social justice helps dismantle the structures that perpetuate hatred. When we work towards creating a more equitable and inclusive society, we create conditions that discourage hatred and encourage empathy.

Leading by Example:
Choosing to respond to hatred with kindness, respect, and understanding sets a powerful example. By embodying the values, we wish to see in the world, we inspire others to do the same.

Be the change you wish to see in the world.
-Mahatma Gandhi

The ant of hatred must be destroyed as soon as it felt within. The curriculum of value education should teach kids to guard their heart. Envelop the heart with so much love and compassion that it becomes impervious to hatred.

CHAPTER 14: Regret

We all make mistakes, have struggles and even regret things in our past. But you are not your mistakes, you are not your struggles, and you are here now with the power to shape your day and your future.
-Steve Maraboli.

Thomas Edison, one of history's most prolific inventors, is often remembered for his philosophy on failure and success, particularly in his quest to invent the incandescent light bulb. Edison faced numerous setbacks while developing the light bulb, experimenting with over 6,000 different materials to find a suitable filament that would burn brightly and last for a reasonable amount of time. Despite these repeated failures, Edison remained undeterred, famously stating, Thomas Edison, one of history's most prolific inventors, is often remembered for his philosophy on failure and success, particularly in his quest to invent the incandescent light bulb. Edison faced numerous setbacks while developing the light bulb, experimenting with over 6,000 different materials to find a suitable filament that would burn brightly and last for a reasonable amount of time. Despite these repeated failures, Edison remained undeterred, famously stating, "I have not failed. I've just found 10,000 ways that won't work."

This relentless experimentation and refusal to give up in the face of failure ultimately led to his success. Edison's breakthrough came when he used a carbonized cotton thread filament, which glowed for over 13 hours. This discovery was pivotal and led to further improvements, including the use of a carbonized bamboo filament that lasted over 1,200 hours. Edison's perseverance and systematic approach to failure not only resulted in the invention of the practical electric light bulb but also set the stage for the modern electric lighting system, fundamentally transforming the world. This relentless experimentation and refusal to give up in the face of failure ultimately led to his success. Edison's breakthrough came when he used a carbonized cotton thread filament, which glowed for over 13 hours. This discovery was pivotal and led to further improvements, including the use of a carbonized bamboo filament that lasted over 1,200 hours. Edison's perseverance and systematic approach to failure not only resulted in the invention of the practical electric light bulb but also set the stage for the modern electric lighting system, fundamentally transforming the world.

This story serves as a light house for those who feel regret at their failed efforts.

Regret, an intricate emotion, has the capacity to haunt our thoughts and stir profound emotions. It is a complex blend of disappointment, remorse, and longing for different outcomes. Regret arises from a sense of dissatisfaction or disappointment with past choices, actions, or missed opportunities. It often accompanies the realization that different decisions could have led to more favorable outcomes. Regret can be triggered by a range of circumstances, such as failed relationships, career choices, or unfulfilled aspirations. It serves as a reminder of our fallibility as humans and our innate desire for improvement.

The Psychological Impact of Regret:

Regret can have a profound psychological impact on individuals. It can lead to feelings of sadness, guilt, and self-blame. Dwelling on regret can also contribute to anxiety and depression, as it keeps us trapped in a cycle of rumination and self-criticism. However, it is essential to recognize that regret, when approached constructively, can also serve as a catalyst for personal growth and positive change.

Regret can trigger Growth and Transformation:

Acknowledging and Accepting Regret:

The first step in harnessing regret is acknowledging its presence and accepting its validity. By recognizing and accepting our past choices and their consequences, we can begin to move forward.

Reflecting on Lessons Learned:

Regret offers an opportunity for self-reflection and introspection. By examining the circumstances surrounding our regret, we can identify patterns, beliefs, or behaviors that contributed to the outcome. This reflection enables us to gain valuable insights and learn from our mistakes.

Pursue Self-Compassion:

While regret can be accompanied by self-blame, it is crucial to cultivate self-compassion. Recognize that everyone makes mistakes, and that growth is a continuous process. Treat yourself with kindness and understanding, allowing room for forgiveness and personal growth.

Making Amends and Act:
Regret can spur us to act and make amends when appropriate. Whether it involves apologizing to someone we've hurt or taking steps to rectify a situation, proactive steps can pave the way for healing and personal growth.
"I have not failed. I've just found 10,000 ways that won't work."
Always remember these lines when you feel low.

Embracing New Opportunities:
Regret can serve as a catalyst for change and open doors to new possibilities. Use the lessons learned from regret to make different choices, pursue new goals, or develop healthier habits. Embracing new opportunities can lead to personal growth and fulfillment.

Regret, although often accompanied by negative emotions, has the potential to be a catalyst for growth and transformation. Rather than allowing regret to paralyze us, let us accept it as a stepping stone towards personal growth, success, resilience, and to a life lived with intention.

CHAPTER 15: Disappointment and Frustration

It was the year 1993. A single mother sat dejected, with tears in her eyes, in a small, cold apartment in Edinburgh. J.K. Rowling, struggling to make ends meet, faced the daunting challenges of unemployment and raising her daughter alone, all while mourning the loss of her mother. Yet, amidst this turmoil, she clung to a flicker of hope: a manuscript about a young wizard named Harry Potter.

Rowling's journey with Harry Potter began during a delayed train journey in 1990, a trip that sparked the creation of a world that would eventually captivate millions. Over the next few years, she poured her heart and soul into writing the manuscript, often writing in local cafés while her daughter slept beside her. This manuscript, however, faced rejection after rejection, with 12 publishing houses turning it down, each refusal a heavy blow to her already fragile state.

Despite the rejections and personal hardships, Rowling's belief in her story never wavered. Her perseverance finally paid off when Bloomsbury, a relatively small publisher in London, decided to take a chance on "Harry Potter and the Philosopher's Stone," influenced by the enthusiasm of the CEO's eight-year-old daughter who, after reading the first chapter, eagerly demanded more.

The publication of the first Harry Potter book in 1997 marked the turning of the tide for Rowling. The series went on to become a global phenomenon, selling over

500 million copies worldwide, translated into more than 80 languages, and inspiring a hugely successful film series, a play, and numerous other ventures. Rowling herself emerged from financial hardship to become the world's first billionaire author.

J.K. Rowling's early years of struggle and disappointment, sitting in that small apartment, could never have hinted at the future that was to unfold. Her story is a profound testament to the resilience of the human spirit, showing how the darkest moments can precede the greatest successes.

Disappointment and frustration are common emotions that arise when our expectations and desires are unmet. While they are natural responses to life's challenges, prolonged or intense experiences of disappointment and frustration can have detrimental effects on our mental and physical well-being. Disappointment occurs when our hopes or expectations are dashed, often leading to feelings of sadness, disillusionment, or discouragement. Frustration, on the other hand, arises from obstacles, setbacks, or the inability to achieve desired outcomes, often resulting in anger, irritability, or restlessness. These emotions can stem from various aspects of life, including relationships, career, personal goals, or unmet societal expectations.

It can manifest in different ways, both mentally and physically. Common symptoms include feelings of sadness, irritability, loss of motivation, decreased self-esteem, difficulty concentrating, and disrupted sleep patterns. Prolonged experiences of these emotions can contribute to chronic stress, which has been linked to various health conditions such as cardiovascular disease, weakened immune function, and mental health disorders like anxiety and depression.

Coping Mechanisms:

Acceptance and Adjustment:
Acknowledge the reality of the situation and accept that disappointment and frustration are normal parts of life. Embrace the idea that setbacks and unmet expectations offer valuable opportunities for growth and learning.

Self-care and Emotional Support:
Engage in self-care activities that promote well-being, such as exercise, healthy eating, adequate sleep, and relaxation techniques like meditation or journaling. Seek support from trusted friends, family, or professionals, as sharing your feelings can provide comfort and perspective.

Shifting Perspectives:
Reframe your mindset by focusing on gratitude and finding silver linings amid disappointment. Practice self-reflection to identify any unrealistic expectations or negative thought patterns that may contribute to frustration.

Goal Setting and Action Steps:
Set realistic, achievable goals to regain a sense of purpose and direction. Break down larger objectives into small, manageable steps, celebrating progress

along the way. Action can help regain a sense of control and motivation.

Seeking Meaning and Purpose:

Reflect on personal values and aspirations. Engage in activities that align with your passions and contribute to a sense of purpose. Volunteering, pursuing hobbies, or engaging in creative outlets can provide fulfillment and a sense of accomplishment.

Disappointment and frustration are inherent aspects of life, but their impact can be managed and mitigated, and they can be transformed for personal growth and a more fulfilling life journey.

CHAPTER 16: Low Self Esteem

Low self-esteem is a pervasive psychological condition that affects millions of individuals worldwide. It is characterized by a negative evaluation of oneself, a lack of confidence, and a diminished sense of self-worth.

Causes of Low Self-Esteem

Early Childhood Experiences:
Negative parenting styles, such as neglect, criticism, or abuse, unrealistic expectations, constant comparisons to others, lack of emotional support or invalidation of one's feelings and opinions can contribute to low self-esteem.

Social and Cultural Factors:
Bullying, peer rejection, social exclusion, media influence, societal beauty standards, discrimination based on race, gender, or other factors can cause low self- esteem.

Personal Factors:
It can also be caused by perfectionism and fear of failure, prolonged periods of stress or trauma, chronic health conditions or physical appearance concerns.

Signs of low self -esteem:
You find it difficult to accept compliments.
You have little trust in yourself.
Talk negatively about yourself.
You lack personal worth and do not respect yourself.
You think that others are better than you.
You think you do not deserve the good things of life.

You feel inadequate and lost.

You compare yourself with others constantly.

You always try to please people.

You survive on the appreciation of others however false they may be.

You let people take advantage of you to feel good about your perceived goodness.

You place others wishes and needs before your own.

You cannot say 'NO'.

You let people walk all over you.

You dread the bad opinion of anyone, however selfish or ignorant they may be.

At the end, you realize that even your life is not your own, for either making or breaking. It is another matter that it just swishes away from your hands.

Thus, low self-esteem makes havoc of our lives. There is a persistent feeling of sadness, anxiety, loneliness, and worthlessness. This increases the vulnerability of developing depression and anxiety disorders. Difficulty arises in managing emotions and establishing healthy relationships.

Behavioral Consequences:

One avoids new challenges or opportunities due to fear of failure. Self-sabotaging behaviors, such as procrastination or self-destructive habits becomes the norm. They withdraw socially and isolate to protect themselves from perceived judgment.

Interpersonal Consequences:

They have difficulty in asserting boundaries or expressing opinions. They attract or remain in toxic relationships. Their communication skills are poor, and they face challenges in building meaningful connections.

Overcoming Low Self-Esteem

Self-Awareness and Acceptance:
It is imperative to recognize negative self-talk and challenge irrational beliefs. Always practice self-compassion and embrace personal strengths. Practice positive affirmations and gratitude exercises regularly.

Building a Supportive Network:
Do not ignore the love you do have in your life by focusing on the love you don't.
-Mandy Hale

How easily we fall into this trap! We crave for that we do not have and what we do have, easily slips away. Time and tide wait for none. Accept the love and life you have with both your hands and arms. Surround yourself with people who appreciate and value you. Engage in therapy or support groups to gain insights and validation.

Developing Coping Strategies:
Set realistic goals and celebrate small achievements. Engage in activities that promote self-care and self-expression. Practice stress management techniques, such as mindfulness or meditation.

Challenging Limiting Beliefs:
Identify and challenge negative core beliefs, engage in cognitive restructuring to replace negative thoughts

with positive ones and recognize that mistakes and failures are part of growth.

Low self-esteem can significantly impact an individual's overall well-being, but it is a condition that can be overcome with dedication and self-reflection.

Those who would love to read in detail about this, can read my book, **'How to Boost Self-Esteem.'**

https://relinks.me/B0CSRQ1N5F

It will hold your hand and guide you through a fascinating journey to high self-esteem.

CHAPTER 17: The Five Sheaths of the Body

In ancient yogic and Ayurvedic traditions, the human body is believed to consist of not just the physical form but also five subtle sheaths, known as the Pancha Koshas. These sheaths are said to envelop the soul and play a crucial role in our overall well- being. Let us understand each sheath and explore ways to keep them healthy.

1. Annamaya Kosha (Physical Sheath):
The Annamaya Kosha represents the physical body, including muscles, bones, organs, and skin. To maintain its health, regular exercise, a balanced preferably vegetarian diet, and sufficient rest are essential. Yoga, meditation, and mindful movement practices can help in keeping this sheath healthy and vibrant.

2. Pranamaya Kosha (Vital Sheath):
The Pranamaya Kosha is the vital energy sheath that governs the flow of prana or life force in the body. Practices like pranayama (breathwork), tai chi, and qigong can help balance and strengthen this sheath. Spending time in nature, deep breathing exercises, yoga asanas and adequate rest are also beneficial for maintaining the vitality of this sheath.

3. Manomaya Kosha (Mental Sheath):
The Manomaya Kosha encompasses the mind and emotions. To keep this sheath healthy, it is important to cultivate positive thoughts, practice mindfulness, and engage in activities that promote mental well-being such as meditation, journaling, and spending time with

loved ones. Managing stress, seeking therapy when needed, yoga asanas and practicing gratitude can also contribute to a healthy mental sheath.

4. Vigyanamaya Kosha (Wisdom Sheath):

The Vigyanamaya Kosha is associated with intuition, wisdom, and discernment. To nurture this sheath, engaging in lifelong learning, introspection, and contemplative practices is crucial. Cultivating self-awareness, seeking knowledge from various sources, and being open to new experiences can help in the development and maintenance of this sheath. Remember the middle -aged man?

5. Anandamaya Kosha (Bliss Sheath):

The Anandamaya Kosha is the innermost sheath representing joy, peace, and spiritual connection. Practices like meditation, prayer, selfless service (seva), and connecting with a sense of purpose and meaning in life can nourish this sheath. Cultivating gratitude, spending time in silence, and engaging in activities that bring joy and fulfillment are essential for maintaining the health of the bliss sheath.

We can achieve **stupendous level of physical and mental well-being** in our lives if the subtle sheaths of the body are healthy and glowing. Integrating practices like 'Kriya Yoga' that purifies the physical, vital, mental, wisdom, and bliss sheaths, can bring a balance and wholeness of the body, mind, and spirit.

EPILOGUE

Dear Reader,

This brings us to the end of our book. Most of the modern system of treatment underscores the importance of mindfulness in controlling and transforming our emotions and thereby the state of the mind. I have been there and done it all. Intense emotions are like waves of an ocean and despite being mighty, it becomes helpless when the moon comes into action. Can you think clearly and mindfully when you are under the throes of an intense one? You just flow along like a helpless twig.

That is why, it is best to practice yoga asanas from an early age. Children should start early. I have seen saint like children who practice them from an early age. But it is never too late to begin. Regular practice keeps your aura glowing and your mind still like the depths of the ocean. Waves on the surface can touch it not.

I could start the purification of my subtle sheaths by the **'Inner Engineering Program'** of the **mystic and Guru, Sadhguru**. It is available online, but it is best to remember that you need to be very regular with the practices to reap substantial benefit. Commit yourself to it only if you are sure that you will be able to spare precious time every day, day after day.

May you able to learn the lessons the negative emotions impart.
May you be able to transform them at the shortest possible time.

May you be able to maintain equanimity of the mind despite the highs and lows.

Life is a roller coaster ride and enjoy it by being an observer. This is a guest house, and we are all here for a short time. We have come here to collect diamonds of wisdom by the varied experiences of our lives. I want my diamonds to be multi coloured like the rainbow. How do you want your collection to be?
Bon Voyage...

Coming Next...

POWER UP
With Yoga

How to BOOST Self Esteem

How to CREATE Positive Emotions

Roses and Thorns Along the Way

A collection of short stories about life

And They Survived

Stories of love, courage, intrigue, and the ultimate triumph of the human spirit

HOW TO BOOST SELF ESTEEM

CONQUE SELF DOUBT, BECOME ASSERTIVE, INCULCATE SELF-LOVE AND SHINE WITH UNPRECEDENTED CONFIDENCE

DR. SAPNA DEB

INTRODUCTION

If you do not love yourself, who will?

There was a pin drop silence in the class of seventh grade students.

The class teacher, Mrs. Mercy John looked at me and repeated, "I want one student from this class to volunteer to read two paragraphs from this English literature book."

I looked down at my feet. A sudden fear had gripped me. My heart was racing. What if I faltered while doing so? Will they laugh at my effort? Will I bring disrepute to my beloved teacher by failing to pronounce the words properly? No, I cannot do this.

Mrs. Mercy continued to look at me for some time and then a deep disappointment spread on her face. This was a school in a small town. A new girl who was from a top-ranking school in a metropolitan city had joined the class recently. She had little regard for the school, teachers, or the students.

Mrs. Mercy had hoped that her brightest student would be able to dissipate the new girl's doubts. She had hoped that her favourite student would validate and prove her teaching prowess.

"Miss, I think it will be better if I read instead of one of them," said the new girl.

She then went about reading in a plain and monotonous voice.

I realized I could have done the same in a far better manner. I was excellent in writing it out on paper. The school was proud of me.

Mrs. Mercy walked away shame faced. I watched her with tears in my eyes.

I met her later when she was alone in her room.

"I am sorry."

"This is what I must show for all the efforts I have put in all these years. Not a single student of mine can hold a candle to an average girl from another school. Was that so difficult a task?"

I left her soon after.

Why was I such a coward? Why did my knees feel weak if I was called upon suddenly in public? Why did I have no confidence in myself?

Alas, I did not have the answers to any of these questions. I did not know how to pull myself out of that rut. I only knew remorse, regret and tears and I wallowed in them until it became my second nature.

I criticized myself, compared myself with others, laughed at myself and regaled friends with anecdotes of my stupidity and mistakes and failures. They laughed and I laughed the loudest at ME. When I came back to my room after that, I wept. I wept silently for that *person who lived inside me, who had no one other than me and whom I seemed to despise*. I thought she was foolish, lazy, silly, and good for nothing. No one loved her and she went out of her way to please people, helped them at the cost of her own welfare, gave away things which she needed the most, so that she could earn praise and recognition. She needed their validation to make her feel good about herself. She needed constant company for she dreaded staying alone.

Such was the need to earn the tag of a 'kind girl' that she did odd jobs for others 'selflessly', thereby wasting precious time. It took a toll on her studies and later, her mental health, her career, her relationships, her physical health, and quality of life.

When you are a doormat,
People will rub their feet on you.

When you are a ghungroo (bell anklet worn while
performing Bharatnatyam dance)
You are worn around the feet,
Even though you are a much loved,
Exquisite piece of creation.

After decades of ignominy and disgrace despite being a successful professional, one day I stood up and said stoically to myself that, "I have had it enough. I refuse to be disrespected and taken for granted."
My life did a somersault since then and kept on doing so till I emerged victorious and shining, brimming with confidence and fearless in every situation.
I now can hardly recognize the OLD me.
 Looking back, I send my love and blessings to my *Old Self and tell her,* that she had always been a Diamond. She had just lost her shine in a slice of time, for I had disowned her.
Whom did she have apart from Me? Who would stand up for her if I didn't? Who could possibly love her when I didn't?
The Universe conspires to give that what you wish, but the wish must be strong enough.
There are things which you can **consciously** do to overcome low self-esteem and then there are those

72

magical things which happen on their own with a few ancient practices. We will learn about both in the following pages.

Human minds have become programmed in such a way that it understands **Logical** reasoning easily. So, we will first explore all that appeals to our left hemisphere. The right hemisphere of our brains can wait.

(Why has been the right hemisphere pushed back into the backstage? Was not enhancing the right first, the logical right choice? The East had always done so…)

It is my sincere wish and prayer that this book of mine, holds your hand gently and takes you along to the light of unshakable confidence.

Bon Voyage…

Low self-esteem is a condition characterized by a negative perception of oneself and a lack of confidence. It is a significant issue that affects individuals worldwide, including the United States and other countries with adolescent and young women being particularly impacted. While data on the extent of low self-esteem globally can be challenging to obtain, studies suggest that it is prevalent across cultures and all age groups.

The detrimental effects of low self-esteem are far-reaching. Individuals with low self-esteem may experience difficulties in forming and maintaining healthy relationships, struggle with academic or professional achievements, and face mental health challenges such as depression and anxiety. Some may evince problem eating, suicidal ideation and multiple health compromising behaviour, especially adolescents.

It can lead to problems such as aggression, anti-social behaviour and delinquency. Moreover, low self-esteem can hinder personal growth and prevent individuals from reaching their highest potential.

Recognizing the impact of low self-esteem, United States and other countries have taken steps to address this issue. Mental health initiatives, including awareness campaigns, educational programs, and counseling services, have been implemented to promote self-esteem and overall well-being. Some schools have incorporated self-esteem-building activities into their curricula to support students' emotional development.

Similarly, other countries, especially India, have also recognized the importance of addressing low self-esteem and affiliated mental health problems. Efforts such as implementing mental health policies, promoting positive body image, and providing accessible mental health services have been undertaken. These initiatives aim to enhance self-esteem and support individuals in developing a positive self-perception.

Efforts are being made to introduce the ancient science of YOGA right from elementary school level.

Assessing the success of these efforts is challenging, as the impact of such initiatives can vary. While some individuals may benefit from the available resources, others may face barriers in accessing them or require more comprehensive support. Additionally, changing societal attitudes and cultural norms that contribute to low self-esteem can be a complex and ongoing process.

Overall efforts to alleviate low self-esteem demonstrate a recognition of its significance and the need to support individuals' mental well-being. However, continuous evaluation, refinement, and expansion of these initiatives are crucial to effectively address the issue and ensure that individuals receive the support they need to cultivate healthy self-esteem.

Out of suffering have emerged the strongest souls.
The most massive characters are seared with scars.
Kahlil Gibran

Ref:
1. R. McGee et.al. Journal of
   Adolescence
2. Dat Tan Nguyen et.al. Frontiers in
   Psychiatry
3. M.Donnellan et.al. Psychological science

CHAPTER 2: Self- Esteem

Nathaniel Branden, the renowned psychotherapist, and writer defined Self-esteem as the **sum of self-confidence and self-respect**. It reflects a person's overall subjective evaluation of their worthiness and abilities.

Self-esteem is an essential component of self-actualization. It refers to the individual's belief in their own **competence and worthiness, leading to a sense of confidence and fulfillment.** This was the view of the American psychologist, **Abraham Maslow.**

Carl Rogers was an American clinical psychologist who was second only to Sigmund Freud. One of the founding fathers of humanistic psychology, he said that Self-esteem is the result of **congruence between a person's self-concept (how they see themselves) and their ideal self** (their desired self-image). It involves **accepting oneself unconditionally** and experiencing positive regard from others.

Albert Bandura was responsible for contributions in the field of psychology, social cognitive therapy, personality psychology and was also the influence between the transition between behaviour and cognitive psychology. According to him, self-esteem is influenced by self-efficacy, which is the **belief in one's capabilities** to accomplish tasks and achieve goals. It involves evaluating one's abilities and performance in various domains of life.

James W. Coleman said that Self-esteem is a sense of **personal worth and value.** It encompasses feelings of self-acceptance, self-respect, and the **belief that one is deserving of happiness** and success.

These definitions highlight the importance of self-esteem in shaping an individual's perception of themselves and their abilities, and how it influences their overall well-being and behavior.

According to me,

Self- esteem is the inherent knowledge within, that one is unique, loved, complete in all ways, capable, has a divine purpose and is an invaluable part of the multiverse.

YOU are special in this creation by the virtue of being born here in this time. There is no other in this universe, who is like you or can replace you.

So, Self- Esteem is a person's overall sense of value, characterized by a positive self-image, a belief in one's inherent abilities, self-love, and a sense of self-worth. It reflects the level of self-confidence, self-acceptance, and self-respect an individual possesses.

It reflects how an individual views and values himself as a human being. People with high self -esteem are confident, smiling, and walk with their heads held high. *"Ye are all Kings," said Jesus.*

Believing in oneself enables one to live and enjoy life. New challenges can be taken on head-on with confidence. One might be good in one area of life but not in the other but integrating them all in the jigsaw puzzle of life will beget happiness and fulfilment.

People with high self -esteem accept themselves as they are, do not compare themselves with others, are realistic, energetic, make clear decisions, have good communication skills, excel in academics, are outgoing, cheerful, have healthy relationships, help others joyously, welcome the unknown, embrace challenges, are resilient and have good physical health and mental well- being.

In other words, they are the 'light' of the world and 'Salt' of the earth.

Your living is determined not so much by what life brings to you as <u>by the attitude you bring to life</u>, not so much by what happens to you as by the way <u>your mind</u> <u>looks at what happens</u>,'
-KAHLIL GIBRAN

CHAPTER 3: Low Self -Esteem

Low self-esteem is a negative perception and evaluation of oneself. It is a subjective and often persistent belief that one is inadequate, unworthy, or inferior. Individuals with low self-esteem tend to have a poor self-image and lack confidence in their abilities, worth, and value as a person. They may constantly criticize themselves, doubt their decisions, and feel insecure in social interactions and relationships.

They often tend to focus on their flaws and shortcomings while disregarding their abilities and achievements. This negative self-evaluation can have a significant impact on various aspects of their lives, including relationships, work or academic performance, and overall well-being.

Low self -esteem can manifest in different ways, such as feelings of self-doubt, constant comparison to others, fear of rejection or failure, melancholy, avoidance of challenges, and difficulty asserting oneself. It can be influenced by a range of factors, including personal experiences, social interactions, cultural influences, and internal beliefs.

In the age of internet when stereotyped ideas are delivered right into the drawing rooms repeatedly, media has started controlling the minds of the present generation. Is it surprising that teenagers around the world dress and eat similarly?

Everyone is part of a herd.

Those with low self-esteem are critical of themselves. They either downplay or ignore their many good qualities. They need someone to point it out to them for they are blind to their own virtues.

They use negative words to describe themselves and feel like failures.

They are judgmental about themselves but not so about others. They consider themselves inferior to those around them.

They talk to themselves (self-talk) in a demeaning manner.

They are self-conscious.

They are compassionate toward others but not towards themselves.

They are not assertive.

They are loving and understanding as regard others, but this virtue is not extended to themselves.

They give the credit of their achievements to luck and others but not to themselves.

They apologize a lot.

They cannot accept a compliment and might consider it to be falsely given.

They tend to blame themselves if things go wrong in the world around them but are too humble to accept credit if things go right.

If you think you can,
You can.
And if you think you can't,
You are right.
Mary Kay Ash

They are usually soft spoken for the fear of causing noise pollution.

They are humble, kind and smiling and the world around uses them to their advantage.

A smile and a kind word can make their day and they will brighten up the day for another at the cost of their own day darkening.

They have difficulty arriving at a decision.

They joke negatively about themselves but become angry when criticized by others.

They find it difficult to make friends.

They would go all out to seek validation to make themselves feel good and are eager to please.

They have the disease of ruminating over past events like a cow. In the process, one past event can make them grieve a thousand times over.

They hand over the goat of their peace of mind to others and then expect to be happy.

They have unrealistic expectations. An unhappy life invites a scourge of diseases, and they traverse the world with long faces.

Let your boat of life be light, packed with only what you need-a homely home and simple pleasures, one or two friends worth the name, someone to love and someone to love you, a cat, a dog, a pipe or two, enough to eat and enough to wear, and a little more than enough to drink: for thirst is a dangerous thing. -Jerome K. Jerome in Three Men in A Boat.

CHAPTER 4: Causes of low self esteem

It was late evening. My father, mother, my sisters, brother, and I were sitting around a small fire. We were listening to the childhood anecdotes of my father. He praised himself lavishly as he spoke. After some time, my mother could take it no more.

"Does anyone praise oneself so?" She asked, embarrassed.

"I praise myself because no one else does so," he answered nonchalantly.

We could not stop laughing at that.

Decades later, when he is no more, I realize the depth of his teaching that day. Laced with humor, he had taught the lesson which would stand at stead for a lifetime.

Do not wait for others to praise you to feel good about yourself. Praise and love yourself, even when others do not.

Afterall, we are our own reward.

There are various factors that can give rise to low self-esteem. Here are some common causes:

Childhood experiences:

A new-born child has left behind a realm where unconditional love is the norm. His memories are still fresh. He craves for that love. If you cuddle a crying child and stroke his back lovingly, he will drop off to sleep. Touch reinforces love and builds a cocoon of warmth and belonging. He realizes that he is loved and is needed and that lays the foundation of self-worth. As he grows older, appreciation and encouragement further strengthen this belief and he grows up into a self-reliant and confident person. On the other hand, negative experiences during childhood, such as abuse, neglect, bullying, or constant criticism, does the opposite and significantly impacts self-esteem later in life.

Unrealistic expectations:
The first three years of childhood is the golden period during which the child needs to fill his receptacle with love of parents, grandparents, and others. Once that threshold is crossed, he carries the bag of expectations on his tiny shoulders to the school. He must excel in whatever he does, be it games or academics. Parents set high standards and at times their own unfulfilled dreams are hoisted on to the shoulders of their children. Add to it the intense competition, and kids have the wind out of their sails from an early age. As they grow up, their own expectations get aligned with that of their parents.

Setting excessively high standards for oneself and feeling constant pressure to achieve them can lead to desperate feelings of inadequacy and low self-esteem.

Once a parent posted a question in social media.

"I want my child to get admission in the Indian institute of Technology. He is five years of age. I am yet to start his preparations for the entrance exam to that institute. Do you think it is already late for that?"

"How could you be so careless? You had to start when he was in the womb, if not earlier. Now, it is already late."

I know not why; I could not stop laughing at the ridiculous answer for a long time.

Social comparison:

Comparing oneself unfavorably to others, especially in the age of social media and photo shoppe, can erode self-esteem as individuals feel they don't measure up to the perceived successes or appearances of others. The latter can be deceptive and maintaining such appearances and perfect Barbie doll bodies is a full-time job. When is the time to do a real full-time job then? A job in which one earns money instead of splurging it...

This comparison breeds two things. Self-pity and jealousy depending on the personality type. Those who are meek and sensitive will admire the achiever and try to emulate. If that is not possible, feelings of self -pity and inadequacy sets in.

In many of the others, jealousy sets in. **Jealousy is a fire which once set alight in the heart, smolders within till it turns its *creator* into ashes.**

It seems strange, but it is true.

Read about this in my next book...

How To CREATE Positive Emotions.

Perfectionism:

Striving for perfection and feeling like any mistake or imperfection is a personal failure can contribute to low self-esteem. Some people think of it as a motivator, but it is not necessarily so.

A desire to achieve can be healthy but a desire to be always perfect is irrational and impossible.

Those who are victims of this seldom have the following.

a. They are obsessed with rules and regulations.

b. They are workaholics and do not give time to themselves to relax.

c. Life just passes them by for they do not enjoy the journey to the achievement.
d. They procrastinate for the fear of not being able to do a job perfectly.
e. Thy have unrealistic standards.
f. They are pushed by a fear of anything which is not near perfect, according to them.

Lack of encouragement:
A lack of recognition, praise, or encouragement during important developmental stages can hinder the development of a healthy sense of self-worth.

Traumatic experiences:
Trauma, such as physical or emotional abuse, failed relationships, financial troubles, can deeply impact self-esteem, leading to feelings of shame, guilt, or worthlessness.

Accepting negative feedback: Taking criticisms and failures to heart and internalizing them as personal flaws can gradually erode self-esteem. People who are sensitive are more prone to this.
Poor academic performance in school results in low levels of confidence. If the parents or teachers are critical, it aggravates the problem.

Cultural and societal influences: Societal pressures, stereotypes, and societal ideals of beauty or success can negatively affect self-esteem, particularly if individuals feel they don't fit those standards.
Chronic illness, severe pain, anxiety, and depression can also cause low self-esteem.

No two flowers are the same and so is life. Every person has a unique life path and a different set of circumstances, situations, and challenges.

The noted psychiatrist and past lives healer, Dr. Brian Weiss indicates through various true stories in his books, that we all choose the situations we are in, to learn life's lessons for advancement of our soul, before our birth. That naturally implies that we have the wherewithal to face every challenge that arises in our lifetime. We just need to delve into our inner strength.

"The world is a gymnasium where we come to make ourselves strong."
-SWAMI VIVEKANANDA

Eliminate negative thinking, banish stress, boost emotional intelligence, and unveil your full potential.

DR. SAPNA DEB

INTRODUCTION

This book will gently guide you through a series of chapters in which you will understand the gamut of emotions, its origin, genetics, and chemistry behind it. Emotions transform as one grows up and in different stages of life, different emotions take center stage. *Not all emotions belong to the realm of the rainbow and the negative uncontrolled ones can create havoc and ravage the life of those who do not teach themselves to hold on to its reins.* Similarly, the *rainbow of positive emotions* can be the harbinger of joy, physical and mental well-being, and perennial peace.

What is the secret of ushering in the rainbow? What can be done to retain it when it dawns into your life? How can one be always mindful of the emotional status and learn to control and regulate it? What are positive emotions? Why should we work towards creating them? What are the effects of these emotions on our body?

You will learn about the negative emotions in detail and dwell on ways to remove them. **Our mind is a wild garden, waiting to be tamed**. The weeds grow on their own and if these are not uprooted, they rage through the garden like a wild fire. Beautiful flowers can be grown only after making space for them first. Plants need to be nurtured with love and care. Have you noticed how swiftly tender new plants wither without it? But is that the case with weeds? They need no care and nurturing, for they thrive on their own.

May your mind be a beautiful garden. May you carry the fragrance and beauty all along. May you find respite, love, understanding and respect in the shade of its trees.
When you have all this within you, you need no one else to make you complete. You then become truly FREE.

You will learn about this and more in the following pages.
Happy reading...

REVIEW REQUEST

Dear Reader,
Thank you very much for buying this book. I wish and pray that this book fulfils your deepest needs and aspirations and guides you on your chosen path.
Please do remember to leave a review.
It is the LIFELINE of one of the roles that I play on this earth, that of an Author.

Chapter 1: Handcuffed

He had come in with handcuffs. Two police officers with guns stood on either side. Three policewomen stood behind.

Once I finished examining the prisoner, I asked one of the officers," Do you have women prisoners too?"

"Yes, there is one," he said pointing to a lady standing behind.

Dressed in same-coloured clothes and in her early twenties, she stood tall, gentle, smiling, beautiful and spoke impeccable English. I had mistaken her as a policewoman.

Once I finished her examination, I could not help asking her, "Why are you in jail?"

"A moment of madness Madam, and it's all over for me."

My heart went out to her. So vulnerable we all become when our emotions are beyond our control.

My mind travelled back to my past. A past in which I was swept away by the flow of a river of unbridled emotions like a helpless twig. It clouded my mind and blinded me to an extent that I now have a past, which is full of regrets, a past the memory of which brings unbridled tears....

If only I had known then that I could control my anger, that I could forgive, that I could transform negative emotions into something beautiful, life would have been so different today.

But an ocean of tears cannot wash away the footprints of the past.

One can only hide the tears, resolve to look back only to remember the lessons learnt and walk the rest of life stoically.

Someday dear reader, I will reveal it all in a memoir.

But can life be joyful despite that pain in the heart? Can it be fruitful despite the loss? Can humanity and the universe benefit by one's mere presence?

The answer is a resounding YES.

Irrespective of your age, it is not too late to embark on this journey. It needs meticulous study, deep understanding as well as diligent practice of the methods of modern medicine and psychology. It needs constant self-awareness. It is a mammoth task if seen as a whole, but simple, if little endeavors and practices are done each day. We will read about them in the following chapters.

But what if all this happens naturally? What if you feel a sudden connection with all that is around, and you become a part of them and they a part of you? What if you realize that all that is, comes from the same source and will ultimately dissolve into the same source? What if you are suddenly overwhelmed with the realization that all that is outside you, are a continuity of you?

What if you connect with the universal consciousness, the superpower, and the Creator?

You become a creator yourself!

Each cell is then overwhelmed with calmness, peace and joy which does not rise and ebb like the waves of the mighty ocean but remains omnipresent in your heart. In such a state of bliss, you expect nothing, for you do not need anything from others. Yours is the world and the universe and everything in between. You celebrate every single moment of your existence in this world and leave the world richer by your very presence. Yes, this is true.

There are centuries old practices which achieve the above. We will delve into a few, from the vast treasure house, which I have learnt and practiced and found useful, and learn about the modern ways to do so too.

CHAPTER 2: The Cup of Emotions

The train was snaking through green valleys and tunnels at a breakneck speed. It was past noon. Despite its speed, the train rocked the passengers to and fro slowly, like a mother rocking her kids to sleep. I was perched on the top berth because of my slight size and agility. Of course, there was nothing to be proud about it for I was ten years old.

I watched the other passengers down below. My mother, father and sisters had not escaped the effect of sleep-inducing slow rocking of the train. The other passengers on the other berths were sleeping too.

The book I held in my hands was enthralling. The books of Enid Blyton were such that once I began reading them, I could not put them down until I had read from the first to the last line. I don't know when my eyes started closing on their own…

A celestial, melancholic voice started coming near. I craned my neck through the edge of my seat but saw no one. It slowly started increasing in intensity and as it entered my being, I dissolved into uncontrollable tears. I searched frantically for money in my bag. By the time I could fish out some, the owner of the voice had proceeded further and had become invisible. I could not stop weeping hours after he had left.

Your world is beautiful,
For all your children to see,
The colors bright and vibrant
Why then do I see nothing?
Unloved and forsaken am I.

The valleys deep and green,
Flows the frothy waters white,
I hear the gentle gurgle,
Why then do I see nothing?
Unloved and forsaken am I.

The Sun glows yellow and bright,
The leaves dance in the breeze,
White wisps of clouds float,
Why then do I see nothing?
Unloved and forsaken am I.

I am your child my God,
Like all the others here,
Why then did you forget,
To put sight in my eyes?
Unloved and forsaken am I.

These were the words of his song. That uncontrolled weeping induced such a catharsis that day, that I became completely empty deep within me and in that emptiness, I touched my core. There is something special about that core.

One who touches it once, gets completely transformed. It is like touching the depth of the ocean by a bubble who then becomes enlightened with the knowledge of its true home. It also becomes humble by the realization that the billions of bubbles all around arise from the same source. In essence, all are one.

Unknown to me, the melodious blind singer had planted a seed in my subconscious, which would decide the course of my future life.

Have you ever been through a similar situation? Were you so overwhelmed with one emotion ever, that it touched the core of your heart and all that was held inside turned into tears and flowed away, making you completely empty?
You start a new life then…

The deeper the sorrow carves into your being,
The more joy you can contain,
Is not the cup that holds your wine the very cup that was burned in the potter's oven?
And is not the lute that soothes your spirit the very wood that was hallowed with knives?
When you are joyous, look deep into your heart and you shall find it is only that which has given you sorrow that is giving you joy.
When you are sorrowful, look again in your heart, and you shall see that in truth you are weeping for that which has been your delight.

-KAHLIL GIBRAN in The Prophet.

CHAPTER 3: Lessons of the Forest

"Nobody is superior, nobody is inferior, but nobody is equal either. People are simply unique, incomparable. You are you, I am I."
OSHO.

I once had a dwelling atop a lonely hill. The beautiful house looked down upon rolling hills on three sides. It had perfectly landscaped garden where flowers and fruit trees abounded. Some dark black rocks jutted out along one of the slopes. They added a touch of wild and a unique touch to it.

Have you ever marveled at the beauty of perfectly landscaped gardens and yet they seemed to lose their charm after some time? Are not most man-made things like that?

In contrast, do you ever get tired of the sunrise or the sunset or the floating clouds in a blue sky? Why is it so? There is exquisite beauty in the untamed.

One day, I walked through one of the adjoining forests on the hills. The winding path was narrow and brown, the trees had zoomed up high and intertwined their hands allowing very little light to filter in. The silence was occasionally broken by the cries of birds and though I was not well versed with the calls of each, it was pure music to the ears.

As I walked further, a raw warmth enveloped me. It was as if the forest was alive and watching me. No two trees seemed to be alike. There was no superiority or inferiority, no beauty and ugliness and no perfect or imperfect among them. They just existed, basking in the sun, and celebrating the glory of their creation. Their mere existence added to the richness of the forest. It was their uniqueness which made them exquisite.

The forest teaches us important lessons. Diversity is beauty and the way of the Creator. The peaceful and the satisfied coexistence of the trees, plants and animals inspire us to celebrate and appreciate the differences amongst us. Why are human beings always trying to conform to a particular standard despite being the most intelligent of all creation?

Imagine if a banana plant wanted to be an apple tree and the apple a jackfruit tree. Chaos would reign and we would be amused.
Each creation is a part of the throbbing fabric of life which is spectacular because of the diversity of its individual parts.
Each one of us is UNIQUE and are here because it has been willed so by the creator. *We defeat the very purpose of our creation when we try to emulate someone else. This is the best time, place, and situation to be in for the advancement of one's soul.*

Read this again and once more. Close your eyes and repeat it. Only when we get the basic knowledge right, will we be able to understand the insights presented in the following chapters. Let this wisdom seep deep within.

In the woods, we return to reason and faith. There I feel that nothing can befall me in life, - no disgrace, no calamity, (leaving me my eyes,) which

nature cannot repair. Standing on the bare ground, -my head bathed by the blithe air, and uplifted into infinite space, -all mean egotism vanishes.
Ralph Wado Emerson

Chapter 4: Exercise 1

Identify a clean and quiet room or a corner. A prayer place where you naturally feel calm and connected to the creator is the best. It is preferable to do this exercise after a cleansing bath with water a few degrees Celsius below room temperature in warmer climates, and water as near the maintained room temperature in cooler climates. Remember to put cold water especially on the crown of the head at the end of the bath.

Wear freshly washed clothes and after seeking the blessings of God, sit on a mat with folded legs. The spine should be always straight during this prayer of affirmations.

I am a special creation of God.
He had made me Unique.
I have been sent here for a purpose.
Each cell within me is throbbing with life.
All that is outside of me is throbbing with life.
The Universe is throbbing with life.
There are spaces between my cells and there are spaces in between all that is created.
That space of the universe flows through the spaces in me.
I make way for the universe to flow through me.
The universe flows through me.
I am one with the universe.
The universe is me and I am the universe.
I am the universe, and the universe is me.
The sun and the moon, the planets and the stars flow through me.

They are in me, and I am in them. They are in me, and I am in them.
I am the universe, and the universe is in me.

Imagine the universe flowing through you in all its power and glory.
An ocean of love flows through you, breaking and dissolving all the barriers you had erected in your heart.
You are light, you are free, you are one with all that is.
Soak in the feeling and hold it as long as you can.

Record these affirmations in your own voice and play it once in the morning and once before you sleep.
Imagine yourself as one with the universe.
Visualization is a powerful way of soaking in the affirmations.

AND THEY SURVIVED

STORIES OF LOVE, COURAGE, INTRIGUE AND THE ULTIMATE TRIUMPH OF THE HUMAN SPIRIT

DR. SAPNA DEB

DEDICATION

This book is dedicated to my little sister, *Sonali Deb,* who is a guardian angel of mine, forever bestowing love from the heavens. Without her, I could never have embarked on this author's journey.

ACKNOWLEDGEMENT

My heart felt gratitude to my mentor and Lighthouse of this role that I play of an author, Mr. Som Bathla.

ACKNOWLEDGEMENT

I remain eternally grateful to my brother Vijay Kumar Dev and my children, Eshaa and Ishaan, who all helped me in various ways.

Made in the USA
Las Vegas, NV
01 April 2025

20395128R00066